ACADEMIC QUALITY MANAGEMENT IN SCHOOLS

DR DHEERAJ MEHROTRA

Contents

PREFACE

***Quality In Academics** defines the job of a teacher, an educator by means of learning to learn as a hobby rather than just being an occasional occurrence. Managing and teaching in a class at school are a science more than an art. The Quality Arena today demands more reflection rather than perfection. The parents today are Smarter than in the gone years and repeatedly they pay emphasis on the Quality of Care and Supervision being guarded to their wards over time. The same phase of the business from the side of the promoter or the principal of the school must see to the strength which otherwise would prove out to be a comparative analysis for the Parents, the ultimate customers to feed their value into the taste of the cake.*

The classroom scenario today demands more experiential experiences and story modes and real-time fascinating teaching environments, unlike my or your years of learning as individuals. With my 27 years of experience in the field of Education, now an Industry has targeted much evidence which brought forward my ignition to compile this as a book.

*I am sure the book, **"Academic Quality***

Management in Schools" *shall certainly come out to be a great PRACTICING TOOL for the educationists further. I invite queries and comments to tqmhead@aol.com*

Dheeraj Mehrotra

Lucknow, INDIA

www.authordheerajmehrotra.com

I

Quality Management in Schools

Hi Friends,

The term QUALITY in Schools means a lot to many.

In any school, the Academic Quality Management System is a flow of guidelines and routine operations designed and drafted to perform and execute the tasks as per the guidelines set by the boards of affiliate or recognition. This set of norms defines a flow of operation to assure a conducive operation within a school of a learning climate with the safety and security of the stakeholders in attendance. The spectrum relates to a few parameters in public, such as Holistic Approach, Experiential & Steam Learning, Qualified & Experienced Faculty, Safe & Hygienic Premises, Handwriting Improvement & Personality Development Sessions and above all, a particular focus on IQ, EQ and SQ.

The set flow of the Academic Quality Management System derives the spectrum of quality parameters, responsibilities, priorities, concerns, mandatory requirements, quality checks, assessment parameters and relevant documentation to assure a fair and acceptable implementation towards the assurance of required satisfaction by the stakeholders in particular.

Quality in School

Quality in a School defines the assurance of all parameters set for a limited and drafted outcome with the best utilities and infrastructure and delivering a Learning Atmosphere where the Climate of meaningful transformation happens as a routine.

Quality in Academics

Quality in Academics is an enhanced operation that activates the novel ways and means of learning as a hobby rather than an occasional occurrence. We as teachers tend to deliver Quality In Academics, assuring the result. Still, it encapsulates the learning that happens and the learning outcome by the end of the session. It is not easy to define the Quality aspect in academics, but we aim for the two words definition "CURE IGNORANCE" and make learning happen. The initiative by schools must be to "CATCH THEM YOUNG AND INNOCENT", for the children are no longer kids but young ADULTS.

The fragrance of Quality in Schools and Academics relates to the stakeholders' satisfaction, particularly Students, Parents, Teachers, and society. The structure of the school and the derivable must be such that Every angle with "Students" should give learning Outcome a preface task as the ultimate inertia to emulate and explore. The fact goes in practice; when ambitions are significant, a strong foundation makes the difference. The guidelines for effective continuous improvement or KAIZEN, in particular, reflect via:

- The root cause needs a deep investigation.

- Identification with significant variations in the outcome.

- Shorter cycle for a planned completion.

To frame a Quality Policy for any school, there has to be a deviated task in mind to attain satisfaction from the side of the Students, Parents and the Teachers with a framework of the learning outcome of a further Five Years to a minimum in mind. The robust diagnosis of the school's functioning should be monitored regularly on day to day expected effects and a planned activity-oriented engagement of every day and every hour of working within the school campus. The management and the student council must reflect the necessary result of the school with the reflection of set MISSION and VISION of the school with a framework of acceptable documented policies and framework for the school's functioning. Schools need to follow the updated guidelines for the best and ultimate school management with inputs from the circulars issued by the respective boards from time to time. It is expected that all schools take meetings and abide by the rules and guidelines set by the authorities and government agencies, making the deliverables safer and smoother and assuring a friendly learning environment.

The recent unfortunate Episodes where the authorities probed many irregularities have put the school leaders on a hot seat with too many conformities on cards every second day of inspection and observation. The quality parameters mentioned here follow the practical guidelines to promote the follow-up, assuring a manipulated set-up religiously.

The planning must reflect the following on priority for all school leaders:

a. *Curriculum Planning*

b. *Teaching-Learning Process*

c. *Approaches to Learning and Teaching*

d. *Student Assessment and Performance*

e. *Co-Scholastic Processes and Outcomes*

f. *Infrastructure- Adequacy, Functionality and Aesthetics*

g. *Human Resources*

h. *Management and Administration*

a. *School Leadership*

j. *Beneficiary Satisfaction*

The pitfalls to be avoided while undertaking continuous improvement projects include:

** Viewing it as a burden daily.*

** Believing that there are no better ways to solve the issues.*

** Improving things does not mean sticking wrongly to what should no longer be done.*

It is worth quoting and learning from Peter Drucker, a management guru, who prescribed enhancing one's skills by initiating small steps than by constantly shooting for the moon. Japanese business language ingrains itself with Kaizen, which means improvement. Quality Circles, PDCA, RCA (5 why), Kanban, Gemba, and Walk, among other tools that can be applied for analysing process improvements, should be abstract to follow in totality.

II

Quality Parameters in a School

In any school, the quality parameters reflect the learning outcome and the safety of the children as one of the top priorities. It has been an excellent task to monitor and evaluate the various set standards to meet the above.

The Effectiveness of School Management

Quality, Safety and Care compete to provide a friendly climate within schools.

Dealing with admission blues to the circulars from the various departments, the real concerns lay at mute, unlike the teachers or the owners at pace. What comes to the united world is the spectrum to manage the learning preview and implementation by doing out the staff of generation of likes for all. The segment of school management has changed over the years, and fascinating the world of learning has improved as well. What lies in the cream of school management is the ultimate joy for the students and safety concern for the parents at the preview to monitor and reflect overall situation—scanning the safety issues dealing with pride to the masses in conjunction with learning to learn as a hobby rather than an occasional occurrence in particular.

The segment relies on the safe monitoring of the school, with the observation of the classrooms and checking the health and hygiene issues on priority. Every school which monitors effectiveness deals with pace to the conjunction of learning to happen and in a verbal educational climate of the school and the classroom with freedom from distractions of any kind and repute. Safety in schools has been a significant concern for the parents, teachers, and school management. The students today have a different form of independence. They believe themselves as young adults rather than just being a child to the preface of mounting learning as a spectrum to deliver at their pride and interpersonal issues. What the kid's desire is the care and the recognition mounting to their satisfaction, among others. The students' council has a great responsibility to deliver towards manipulating all the government of school concerns. The safety spectrum lies with no touch either in isolation; the feedback controls with greater emphasis on routine activities and supervision. The perfect duties, including the lunch break duties on the floors, the school over task and above all the classroom management duties including that of the switchboard in charge and chalk and duster recognition scribes the inventory of the responsibilities in order.

Literature Review on Safety Net:

Being an educator, I reflect the management by the authorities towards the effective schooling contributes to the safety of major. The issues which appear to mount with the march of time effectively deal with the monitoring of the whole affair, including the dispersion of the students for home or for labs or even for the assembly, every time there have to be defined exit and entry points with specified staircases to manipulate the success stories at dense priority for the masses. Looking at the dwelled capsules of set-up within schools, we need to go away with the compromising decisions that turn violent and result in heartaches, not headaches that generally would have been tolerable. The concept of school management has had its turn face from Security and Safety as one of the ultimate goals to populate the masses. We need to nurture healthy minds, and there have to be measured to help get every student's unique psychological needs via the collaboration of Teachers and Parents at large. The priorities which need to explore include the maintenance of Health Cards as envisaged by the Comprehensive School Health Programme of the board, the upkeep of the medical records of students with particular health problems and a check on the school to assure that the teachers have undergone introductory training/ bridge courses on counselling, first-aid and identification of disabilities/ learning difficulties.

Keeping the pace given the concern towards the safety, the schools are advised to govern and explore the health climate to be fostered and evaluated regularly. The laboratories and other classrooms need to be equipped to handle the common emergencies. There has to be a strict vigil and control over the building by outsiders/ visitors. The secluded corners, corridors, and staircases are kept under watch by staff members during the lunch breaks and at dispersal time. As per the guidelines of the CBSE, the physical education instructors, too, need to be sensitive enough to involve students in sports according to their physical capabilities and health-related issues. In addition, it is indeed a mandatory affair to have a strong policy statement against child abuse and exploitation. Hence, there is a need to check the background history of the staff before they are allowed to work with the children. Let there be regular sessions on 'good touch and bad touch, and the children need to be helped to understand their rights over their body, especially the right to say "No", as a priority.

The 'Ryan' episode has made all ignored practices in the limelight, and hence we need to come to pose the same as a priority keeping the grave concern from taking an ugly turn. The schools need to provide a sensitive platform through governance for building self-esteem and communication skills among the children. The core idea should be to 'Nurture Knowledge and Deliver Values'. I recall the speech of Neil O'Brien, Former Chairman, CISCE, "Don't cover the syllabus, uncover the syllabus. Give children what they need. Let us invite and involve people to change and innovate. We need to look at matters in Schools of today slightly differently. Schools need to bring in a corporate structure within their perspective set up. They need to bring in an administrator, an HR, a marketing officer, for the man who is the best Administrator may not be a good Academician". This certainly reflects a mounting diagnosis for the management of the school effectively.

In addition, as per the former minister of Law and Justice of India and of HRD and Minister of Communications and IT, Government of India, Kapil Sibal, "There is an urgent need to shift from the earlier paradigm of an education system that was linear, passive, hierarchical, non-participatory, to a system that is dynamic, vigorous and bold: inclusive and integrated; focused on cultivating creativity and intellectual skills; aligned to the needs of the sub-system of Indian society: geared to provide vocational or technical or professional education required in the global workplace and it is here that the Government and society count on the wisdom of the Management, Principals and Teachers of schools to step in.

To deliver the pact of delivery within schools, Quality must be given a preferred seat as progress is impossible without change, and those who cannot change their minds cannot change anything, says George Bernard Shaw. Therefore, the education delivery is poised for a revolutionary change in its approach and methodology. Innovation must play a role within classrooms, probably starting with the ages-old seating arrangement, with the ROW and the COLUMN with some innovative interface style. In addition, the ruptured Chalk and the Duster must change to smart touch boards on priority as it is high time we go for it. In this age of accelerating and mass change at all levels, we have to figure out the ideal strategies and implement them at levels to harness quality as a HABIT rather than an occasional occurrence!

III

Academic Priorities

The school management has to deal with so many responsibilities and priorities on the move through directions and communication.

The Class Inspections and frequent rounds by the head of the school monitor practical evaluation as a continuous process.

The modules relate to:

- Lesson Plan for the day

The lesson plan must have acquaintance among the Principal and Staff with the NCF (National Curriculum Framework) document.

Seminars need to be conducted concerning the NCF.

Teachers need to be encouraged to go through the NCF as a documentary ready reckoner for classroom management.

NCF has to be integrated into total like WORKING the talk.

- Weekly Lesson Plan Diary

Proper documentation with learning outcomes and course/ content completion reports involves the pace.

- Daily Work Programme

This includes the daily analysis and the planned classroom routine. I need to have a recap on regular terms.

- Presentation

Every teacher/ student has to use the power of technology and tools available to enhance the children's learning. The presentation with excellent communication skills is a priority for all teachers to create a WOW moment of classroom learning.

- Teaching Aids/ SmartBoard Used

The utility of Smart Boards needs to be emphasised, and teachers must be told to make effective use of these boards to bring interest in the learning complexities of the children. Multimedia is the in thing, and schools have a significant investment in these tools to deliver effective learning outcomes.

- Students' Response

Regular Parents-Teachers meetings and connectivity via WhatsApp groups or class diaries is a common requirement for any class to have a response mechanism. Parents should be encouraged to have an interface towards the children's learning outcomes and their connection with the teachers.

- Class Work & Home Work

An analysis of every classwork and the homework should be documented for setting up norms and policies. A drafted homework policy must be in its place with a framework of recap and evaluation. This also checks the proper and timely correction work by the teachers.

- Any Special Project/ Demonstration

Every school has set guidelines to follow from the side of the deliverables from the board of education concerned. It is expected to have groups/ clubs/ activities on selected dates/ days/ occasions to monitor the continuous evaluation of the students.

- Communication & Effectiveness in delivery

Communication plays an active role at all levels of school management. Any decision making or conclusion, or even a promotion of a child, activates with the system's effectiveness. A particular framework and SMS (School Management System) has to be in its place for proper functioning. Various ERP – Enterprise Resource Planning- based software are available. Still, adequate implementation has to be at its site with nomenclature fields and customised fields to reflect an accurate and organised report for evaluating the scope for betterment.

The connection with the parents is vital from the end of the SMS- from being absent in the class to the approach of intimation regarding the postponement of the test scheduled or the child's nomination for a student council, seeking a no-objection Y/N from the parent. The effectiveness of the connection and communication with the parents activates the normal functioning of the school with no or most minor complaints from the side of the parents, who otherwise become the most significant strain on the school's management in order.

IV

Tackling Google Generation within classrooms

The Quality Requirements of Google Generation Today!

Google Generation, the ultimate Classroom Scenario, provokes the teachers to take a more significant step today towards promoting themselves in a big way.

Scratching heads and making the designs with the pen or the pencil in the class is a common sight in a classroom today if it is not mounted and reflected by the sense of e-effect, the electronic fur at the school. The distraction in the school otherwise is expected to roll out with a particular launch of the spectrum towards working or phasing out the teaching and learning environment. What evaluates this methodology is the systematic approach toward working for the better to deliver the good out of the best.

The very use of technology in classrooms is changing everything from how pupils learn and how teachers teach to the way parents and teachers communicate. There has to be an updated broadband connection to the Internet to make it possible for growing schools to provide the Quality Base and Information of Learning with a comic effect that further details the information towards the children's liking in particular. The emphasis is on the requirements that promote the Smart Learning Environment, which offers the students and the staff access to all the resources, online storage, and communications tools they could ever need - not just during the school day but beyond it. Further, the New technologies go way beyond paper and pencil to enable children to express themselves textually, graphically, numerically, aurally or visually and allow children to discover new ways to collaborate and learn. As a matter to observe and ponder over, in a national survey, teachers believe that using digital games in the classroom helps students maintain concentration and enthusiasm for learning while making it easier for teachers to differentiate instruction and assess students. The survey of 505 teachers who use digital games in their K-8 classrooms aims to identify what teachers think about game-based learning and how digital games affect students beyond academic achievement. It offers a mix of qualitative interviews with quantitative data to provide a more rounded picture of teacher opinions.

As we are not well outdated and unreferenced with the tab that Digital natives and digital immigrants are terms coined by the American futurist Marc Prensky to distinguish between those who have grown up with technology and those who have adapted to it, there is an urgent need and analysis of when and how we need to change ourselves to the existing scenario and get to the bargain price of Changing with the environment and the opportune moment otherwise. There is a severe need for perfection bound to produce our existence otherwise with a tag of Old Generation buddies otherwise like that of a civilisation hence.

The requirements, as we know from observation, the overall, learning today is much more interactive than it used to be. On priority, the very Learning has had become significantly richer as students have access to new and different types of information, they can manipulate it on the computer through graphic displays or controlled experiments in ways never before possible, and they can communicate the results of their efforts to teachers through a variety of media. We need to involve them, make them a learning partner, and explore their creativity further. New ways of obtaining and presenting information have given students powerful new ways of analysing and understanding the world around them. Research also shows that children who use technology to support their learning are more motivated and engaged.

With clarity and congestion, education is increasingly infused with media content, which can distract students by leading them into too many conflicting directions at once, discouraging their commitment to any one path. Teaching ethics and international relations in the classroom without borders is a commitment to our growth as human beings in a world in desperate need of humanity during a moral crisis. Classrooms today are more diverse than ever before. The same cannot be said about textbooks, curricula, and lesson plans. Teachers must design lessons accessible to all students and reflect their diversities. One has to explore different approaches to traditional learning systems and find out how to implement new strategies to engage students in lessons. The teachers of the new age of Demand and Liking need to be open to ADAPTING, Being Visionary towards perfection, Collaborating with choice and energy with sharing routine operations towards the betterment of ease and fraternity, and keeping the audience in mind. They need to be modelling behaviour, must be leading, open to taking risks, and keen to learn. In addition, the Quality Educator also models tolerance, global awareness and reflective practice, whether it is through the quiet, personal inspection of their teaching and learning process or through blogs, Twitter and others.

It is alarming to note and analyse the fact that, according to researchers, we are in the midst of a sea change in the way we read and think. Our digitally native children have wonderfully flexible minds. They absorb information quickly, adapt to changes and are adept at culling from multiple sources. But they also have internet-induced attention deficit disorder. The quality culture today demands with perfection the art and artistic attitude of the teachers, which in a flash to make the best of efforts and pride culture within the classrooms in a big way. There is an urgent need to answer the google generation today, and for this, one has to be more INFORMED and calculated towards knowledge these days.

V

The New Normal

To Teach is to preach. The subjective modulation task the learning regime to years and years of research with leverage of connecting within the learners. Teach children to teach themselves, and foster a love for learning. So, why are there so many students who cave in and quit? Why are the student dropout rates at an astonishingly high rate? Whatever happened to parental involvement and budgets that generally supported a solid, quality education?

To the pride of learning, I ask, what are students expected to learn from their classroom experiences? What do they genuinely need to know to be successful and prepared for college or career readiness? Current research shows that Deep Learning and Close Reading techniques significantly improve academic results for all students involved. How do we, as educators, foster these and other research-based programs in more schools? Quality instruction is a vital component of quality education; however, not all learning is acquired and grasped inside the classroom environment. Indeed, teachers should encourage students to explore, be critical thinkers, and become learner-centred. An exceptional teacher focuses on classroom teaching, community building, and individualised mentorship.

The time says it all; the page is sure with the inception of technology in education. However, irrespective of the perseverance, determination and aptitude of highly qualified educators, ultimately, students will get out of their education what they put in. The philosophical dilemma doesn't exist with the concept of inspiring the already gifted students or edifying the students who have a passion for learning. The true challenge of teaching is engaging and nurturing the love of learning for all students, especially those who have academically and emotionally "checked out". The solace remains towards bringing learning within the four walls of the classrooms from the BLACK SCREENS of the kids, desktops, laptops and now the palmtops via mobile. Students need to attain more than rigorous content objectives. There needs to be a paradigm shift towards less palpable skills and a greater emphasis on creative thinking, collaboration and problem-solving coupled with thorough teaching and instruction. Students will primarily benefit when they reflect upon and evaluate ways to improve their overall comprehension. Teachers should also seek beneath and beyond the expectations of standards to teach the whole child. As a lifelong learner, I delight in being the student and the teacher. I embrace the challenges of pedagogy and an academic arena of active learning and teamwork. Within quality instruction and education, the framework is the need for real-world experiences, discussions, analysis, and evaluations.

Far to believe but for sure, Engaging students to be equipped to grasp the material, embrace technology and facilitate classroom dialogue strategically is the pinnacle. The crux of my educational and professional endeavours has fashioned my teaching perspective, and ultimately, students should be at the core of all teaching philosophies. The aim towards Creativity within classrooms activates with the perception of engagement with all the kids and not just with the few bright minds. The initiative has to be to catch them young and innocent. It is high time that we approach the mechanism to Teach One- Teach All as a prime scope towards gaining connection with the kids in the classrooms. The children engage and tend to RUN away from Teachers they don't like.

They only want the subject if they like the teachers. Hence, it is requisite for all the teachers to bring in a **WOW** *capsule expose' within and outside the classrooms incorporated through creativity and spectrum of learning to learn as a hobby rather than an occasional occurrence. Let learning be creative, experiential and above all, fertile.*

Educators need genuine criticism. A positive school culture begins with:

- *Sustaining great contemplations.*
- *A decent morning gathering.*
- *Positive reasoning of guardians and instructors.*
- *No business approach*
- *The assistance of positive reasoning of the Principal, instructors and guardians who establish a positive climate to improve the understudies and the general public.*
- *Care*
- *Trust*
- *Establishing a positive climate around.*
- *Positive Morning*
- *Positive educators*
- *Committed work of the instructors*
- *Disposition*
- *Positive and imaginative reasoning.*
- *Discipline.*
- *A solid group with trust, care and love for one*

another.

- *A solid and positive cooperation.*
- *Appreciation.*
- *Normal head.*
- *Love to understudies*
- *Blissful Children*
- *Correspondence*
- *Schooling past books and hypotheses.*
- *Esteem schooling*
- *Strengthening and regard.*
- *How we treat one another.*
- *Positive school the executives advisory group.*
- *Mindful Parents and a delicate school the executives.*
- *Everybody, Principals, educators, guardians and understudies.*
- *Everybody's development.*
- *Positive is educating in the positive air with positive contemplations and examinations.*
- *An enthusiastic educator and humane administration.*
- *Committed, selfless, learned and positive facilitators.*
- *Cherishing, mindful and excited instructors.*
- *Appreciation.*
- *Love and information ought to be granted to the understudies by a positive educator.*
- *Uplifting outlook to bestow information.*
- *Blissful Environment.*
- *Pure confidence in educators.*
- *Winning connections.*
- *Moving statements and supplication.*
- *Positive individuals.*

• Uplifting perspective.
• Positive considerations.
• Cooperation.
• An energetic instructor. A decent instructor affects the cerebrums of children. What is planted early has profound and solid roots.
• Positive pioneer.
• Head.
• A cheerful youngster.
• A warm and cheerful grin.
• Love, fondness and belongingness.
• Persistence.
• Positive resources.
• With rockstar instructors.
• Zero, and afterwards, you move towards the right on the number line.
• Bliss
• Positive nurturing, positive educators.
• Positive individuals.
• Anxious to welcome the educators.
• A beautiful chime sound toward the beginning of the day.
• Sympathy and a feeling of belongingness.
• Positive Thought.
• Positive instructors like us all.
• Everything starts at home.
• Learning.
• Opportunity to share your fantasies.
• Inspiration.
• Discipline.
• Self
• Uplifting outlook
• Quality Education. Positive reaction from

understudies.

VI

Academic Audits & Appraisals

Quality at the workplace has been a thing of demand by the majority. Its inception has been of reputation by the Parents, the ultimate stakeholders, including the students and society. The particular conjunction with the need delivers a demand to pursue a quality learning environment that otherwise remains to a limit only.

The class organisation and the opportunities to the children given within the classroom by the teachers pertain to the existing norms and liking of the teachers at pace in particular. Also, the factors which influence the need for audit limit to planning for continuity and progression in learning, match of work to student's needs, interests, and the clarity of objectives without which the tots do not feel at home within the four walls. Above all, the teaching tools in practice need to be evaluated regarding whether the usage during the lesson is appropriate or not. With this, the teachers' subject knowledge, enthusiasm, questioning methods, exposition, and problem-solving related to the multilevel dimension for judging. Also, whether the work is tailored to individual needs or not is a concern for parents and the management of the school.

As rightly judged and defined by the researchers, Schools need to switch from academic excellence to overall excellence. This can be done only if we re-engineer the human resources available to the teachers. They have to be retrained to the modern aspects of multimedia technology and the current thinking in education. The classrooms must be made centres of excellence.

It is required to judge the following factors in particular on priority:

a. *Curriculum Planning*

b.

Teaching Learning Processes

c.

Student Assessment and Performance

The Teaching-Learning Process forms the basis of the educational process and products. The need for Quality Assessment is a novel way by the Central Board of Secondary Education to pave the delivery in the best possible manner. It relates to the following objectives, viz.

- *To assess and endorse that an institution/ school meets established standards.*

- *To assess the effectiveness of an institution in creating the most innovative, relevant, socially conscious eco-oriented learning ambience for all its staff and students.*

- *To involve the faculty comprehensively in institutional evaluation and planning for enhancing the effectiveness of a school.*

-

- *To establish criteria for professional certification and upgrading of standards.*

- *To encourage continuous self-assessment, accountability and autonomy in innovation in school education.*

- *To encourage continuous professional development and capacity building of teachers.*

This type of audit or an assessment is intended to be a means to document the strengths and weaknesses of educational practices and institutional effectiveness, leading them to the desired accountability towards the society and the stakeholders further. The process is bound to entertain issues related to the school's strengths with areas of development, professional skills, and upliftment required and the classroom management format of demand.

VII

Quality Circles Within Classrooms

The term Quality Circle is a group of members who get together in a circle and sit and brainstorm over a work-related problem; they analyse, identify and discuss strategies and solutions for its implementation. The history of Quality Circles is related to JAPAN as the first country to have introduced this concept to its workers. It was more like a voluntary activity to identify the work-related problems and develop solutions to the same through various tools of the Quality Circle methodology. With the introduction of this quality philosophy of the Japanese, the country rose like a phoenix after the devastation of the second world war. The practice of this concept under the umbrella of KAIZEN gave pace to monitoring the quality practices and development of the nation.

QC in Academics has had its pace through the introduction of Quality Circles during the early 1990s' with the inspiration of Quality Enthusiast Dr Jagdish Gandhi, who, on his return from Japan, introduced the idea of Quality Circles in his school at City Montessori Schools, Lucknow, in India. Dr Vineeta Kamran, one of the heads of his schools, along with the help of P.C.Bihari and S. Das, introduced this concept as a practice of learning and teaching in classrooms ever since the idea of Quality Circles became a craze for schools towards excellence as a joint initiative.

Slowly and steadily, the concept enriched the interest of school leaders in other countries too. The schools from Nepal, Sri Lanka, Mauritius, UK, USA, Pakistan and Bangladesh took the lead through the First International Convention On Students' Quality Circles way back in 1997 at Lucknow, India. Ever since the inception of Quality Circles has garnered priority within schools, and NEPAL has introduced it as a subject in their school curriculum, to the surprise of many. This has been one of the revolutionary steps to promote the cause and concern towards Quality Awareness within schools.

Recently, the year 2017 celebrated two decades of this concept within schools through the participation of over 500 delegates at the 20th International Convention on Students' Quality Circles- 2017, which was organised from 14th to 19th May, at Embilipitiya, Sabaragamuwa Province of Sri Lanka, in collaboration with the Ministry of Education, Information Technology & Cultural Affairs and Department of Education. The convention's theme was " Students' Quality Circles as an Integral Part of Total Quality Management in Education." It proved to be an excellent opportunity for the students, teachers, principals and quality enthusiasts to build knowledge of each others' country, people, culture and language and acquire global awareness and skills so crucial to living and working in the worldwide village, creating long-life friendships across cultures, rightly commented by Herath P. Kularathna, Chief Secretary- Sabaragamuwa Province, & Director General (WCTQEE), Sri Lanka.

The chief minister of the host nation, Mahiepala Herath, of the recently concluded ICQC, quotes on importance of Quality Circles, "I strongly believe that this convention brings the students from different cultures, regions, religions, languages and colour to come under a single umbrella to make a single globe by sharing and exchanging their views, ideas and knowledge and will provide an opportunity to students of different countries to compete on a common platform which will strengthen the understanding and communication among youths from different countries, promoting friendship around the world and cultivating the spirit of teamwork and cooperation." The convention proved to be an excellent nurturing platform for the student delegates who participated actively in various activities, including the "Quality Circles Case Study Presentations". The Quality Circle concept in academics plays a vital role in the overall development of the students with a wide range of learning spectrum in the process. The kaizen philosophy of continuous improvement is the cult behind the QC concept, and the initiative is to cure ignorance as to the ultimate objective among the students.

As discussed above, a Quality Circle is a group of people who assemble in a circle and brainstorm over a particular topic belonging to their work area and try discussing the strategies, causes and solutions and accordingly try implementing an answer. A Student Quality Circle, also known as SQC, is a group of 5 to 15 student members; an ideal number is 8, who sit together in the form of a circle and discuss work-related problems. Accordingly, they evaluate the causes of the selected issue, try to solve the same using the various quality tools, and finally develop strategies to plan and execute the derivatives.

Steps required to frame a Student Quality Circle:

- *Formation of a group of 5 to 15 members.*
- *Selection of the Leader of the Group.*
- *Nomenclature of the Group.*

- *Facilitator/ Teacher/ Advisor of the group*
- *Brainstorming Sessions*
- *Periodic Meetings*
- *Issues being discussed.*
- *Selection of the problem.*
- *Identification and Review of the problem.*
- *Identification of the Causes of the selected problem.*
- *We are implementing TOOLS of problem-Solving.*
- *Evaluation of the Case Study.*
- *Development of Strategies.*
-

Implementation of Strategies.

•

Sharing/ Observation of outcomes.

•

The scenario of Quality Circles frames the inception and implementation through a process of mainly three to four months. It may re-occur with the frame to take another problem or concern by the group. In every change of project objective, it is recommended that the leadership changes from one member to the other. Ideally, the number should be eight and all should work as a team with an equal share of responsibilities and concerns.

Keeping the members' contribution in view, the duties are divided during the case study presentation before the school management/ school assembly, which further promotes the shared objectives and strategies to become a practice for the others to emulate as a norm. The aim is to promote a quality culture of "Making Students Street Smart".

VIII

Managing via Design Thinking

The approach of design thinking is innovation through collaboration. The change of the learning preferences is on the cards with the spectrum of new age challenges and the tech world learners who have complex concerns in understanding and learning. Design Thinking encapsulates a human-centred approach to problem-solving that begins with developing empathy for those facing a particular challenge. Design Thinking is a process for solving complex problems in particular. It is all about kids taking ownership of their education. Its Wikipedia page, which enthusiasts wrote, defines the term: "Design Thinking refers to creative strategies designers use during designing. Design Thinking is also an approach that can be used to consider issues, with a means

to help resolve these issues, more broadly than within professional design practise and has been applied in business and social issues."

It was adapted for business purposes by Faste's Standard Colleague David M. Kelley, who founded the design consultancy IDEO in 1991. Further, Richard Buchanan's 1992 article, "Wicked Problems in Design Thinking", expressed a broader view of design thinking, addressing intractable human concerns through design.

Design thinking is generally defined as an analytic and creative process that engages a person in opportunities to experiment, create and prototype models, gather feedback, and redesign. In academics, it explores the nurturing of talents in a big way.

In addition it draws steps relating to:

Empathy ==> Define ==> Ideate ==> Prototype ==> Test

The follow up within classrooms sound to the very lamination of the above steps concerning manipulation. It seeks to foster collaboration and peer interaction. It also permits students and teachers to personalise the learning by tailoring its offerings to their learning style, career goals, current knowledge and personal preferences.

The above five steps of design thinking laminate innovation while working and solving issues, leading to a better perception of an idea and the initiative. Hence, it is a five-step process to develop meaningful ideas to solve real problems for a particular group of people. It is a mindset and an approach to learning, collaboration and problem-solving.

The aim is to negotiate the mind and preferences to aim at excellence. It is well set towards the spectrum via the PDCA- The Plan, Do, Check and Act supervision by the Deming Cycle and the DMAIC- Define, Measure, Analyse, Inspect and Control mechanism of the Six Sigma methodology towards process management and solving problems in academics in particular. A process with a structured framework for identifying challenges, gathering information, generating potential solutions, refining ideas and testing solutions in particular. As a methodology, designers use it to solve complex problems and find desirable solutions for clients. It draws upon logic, imagination, intuition, and systemic reasoning to explore possibilities of what could be and create desired outcomes that benefit the end-user, i.e. the customer.

Principles of Design thinking reflect upon complex problems and draft desirable solutions. The process is taught in design and business schools worldwide, with schools no exception. The study, published in the Journal of Learning Sciences on April 15, found that students applied the strategies they had learned to entirely new problems without prompting and performed better on projects. Notably, the most significant benefits went to low-achieving students. Doris B. Chin and Kristen P. Blair of the H-STAR Institute at Stanford GSE led the research. "The overall takeaway is that we were able, through instruction, to change the way students were able to approach problems," said Chin. "The strategies we thought would be good are good, and the kids are choosing to transfer them from classroom instruction to a different environment."

To improve the design thinking, one has to observe the exercises, talk to people being surveyed, Brainstorm via ideation, mind mapping, prototyping and draw upon logic, imagination and systematic reasoning. Our motto is 'Student First.' We, as educators, believe in becoming a catalyst in public-private efforts and raising the quality of learning outcomes across schools to ensure that no child is left behind. Students obtaining design thinking abilities can distinguish and foster imaginative and clever fixes to issues when they face them. As a result, the students tend to change as hopeful, compassionate, and in a process, learn and explore tackling the complex difficulties of the approaching future.

IX

Digital Tools For Teaching

The essence of Technology identifies learning, and the digital revolution has paced the march of success with the presence of cloud-based computing and deliberations. The nurturing of understanding is encapsulated using the power of technology with WWW- providing learning at pace out of a click of a button at What Ever, When Ever and Were Ever to the surprise of many. Some of the fascinating tools for teaching related to the usage of MS Office at density, with PowerPoint nourishing the majority of the teachers in totality. Still, perfection has to have the stroke of success with the acceptance from the side of the children in particular.

Well, teachers, the ppt days are over and dead with the lamination of the AI, and the AR segmentation is stated as Artificial Intelligence and Augmented reality in order. The digital lessons provide a sound base with the incorporation of the tools which sound fine with a little hands-on by the teachers but relate to the individual cloud presence by the teacher and a lot of ORM- Online reputation management figure out to the density of understanding and related energy syndrome of clarity among the students at large.

Some of the fascinating and modern applications which relate to the contribution by the teachers figure out for Teaching the Future with the adoption of technology which heavily goes beyond the social networking so-called FACEBOOK and GOOGLE SEARCH options. The incorporated tools for the teachers replicate the understanding and the learning in mass through the doses of the following:

a. *Social Networking and Collaborations:*

The tools here include:

i. *Wikispaces- May be used by teachers to create their Wikispaces to share the teaching and learning materials along with the daily lessons.*

ii. *Schoology- Used to allow teachers to manage their lessons and engage students.*

iii. *Pinterest- Used to generate assignments, projects and lesson plans.*

iv. *Edmodo- Used as a social networking site.*

v. *Skype- Used for video calling and webcasting.*

vi. *Quora- Used for discussions.*

vii. *Udemy- Used for course uploads and learning.*

a. *Enhancing the Pedagogical Processes with websites in demand like the following:*

i. *Khan Academy- This allows sharing of videos and lessons on various subjects.*

ii. *FunBrain- This allows games on Maths and Logical Reasoning.*

iii. *Animoto- This allows teachers to create simple video-based presentations for the class.*

iv. *Office 365 for Education: Allows free email, shared documents, storage and documentation.*

v. *Kodu- A tool for teaching programming, problem-solving and collaboration in a creative hands-on environment.*

vi.

Teleport- It is a tool which allows downloading all or a part of a website to your computer enabling browsing directly from your hard disk.

vii.

Youtube Downloader- This is a fascinating tool which allows downloading any youtube video for further viewing and sharing.

viii.

Yenka- A tool which provides 3Ds experiments and models for mathematics, science and technology.

c.

Planning Lessons and Projects, attribute to the following tools,

i.

Prezi- A tool for developing presentations.

ii.

Planboard- A tool to enable planning and managing daily lessons.

iii. *Google Docs- Allow sharing documents with modifications by any user logged in.*

iv. *Youtube- A tool which allows videos to be uploaded or downloaded on various topics and tastes.*

v. *TEDx is a stand-alone channel with thousands of real-life videos on innovation and activation.*

vi. *Photosynth- This helps students learn through interactive 3D experiences.*

vii. *meeting- This is a great way to connect and carry out teaching. It is the most powerful web conferencing solution for education, training, meeting webinars and tech support.*

d.

Building a Digital Database is possible via the use of the following tools:

i. *Evernote: It is an app designed for note-taking, organising, task lists and archiving.*

ii. *Twitter: It is a great platform and a networking service for posting ideas and thoughts with a limitation of words. Tweets are the posts which people share on Twitter.*

iii. *Scribd: This is a platform to access everything and anything as information. One may post or upload data and share it on other social websites.*

iv. *Slideshare: This tool allows uploads of presentations and search information related to presentation format and can also be downloaded.*

v. *G Suite (Google Apps for Education)- offers many functions, including Gmail, Calendar, Classroom, Contacts, Drive,*

Docs, Forms, Groups, Sheets, Sites, Slides and Hangouts, of great use by the teachers and the schools in particular.

The recruitment is towards catching them young and innocent to the fertile theory of understanding. Majorly, the teachers need to be aware of the above usage in practical implementation and relationship towards execution.

In addition, during the last couple of years, technology was used to plan and execute our lessons through various online platforms like that Wordwall, Getepic, Go Formative, Flipgrid and many Google Apps. This led to more tech as a base for teaching than the ordinary chalk and talk.

Happy Computing and Cyber-based teaching! is the new normal for all teachers, with NEP 2020 promising an undeniable change both to how content is imparted and in which students engage with the learning process as a whole. NEP 2020 recommends that there should be no rigid separation between Art and Science, Academic and Co-curricular learning. This is already being done at all schools through collaborative learning via technology integration as a priority.

About The Author

Dheeraj Mehrotra, MS, MPhil, PhD (Education Management) honoris causa., a white and a yellow belt in SIX SIGMA, a Certified NLP Business Diploma holder, is an Educational Innovator, Author, with expertise in Six Sigma In Education, Academic Audits, Neuro-Linguistic Programming (NLP), Total Quality Management In Education, an Experiential Educator, a CBSE Resource towards School Assessment (SQAA), CCE, JIT, Five S and KAIZEN. He has authored over 40 books on

Computer Science for ICSE/ ISC/ CBSE Students and over 50 books of academic interest for the field of education excellence and Six Sigma. A former Principal at Dc Indian Public School, New Delhi, (INDIA) with an ample teaching experience of over Two Decades, he is a certified Trainer for Quality Circles/ TQM in Education and QCI Standards for School Accreditation/ Six Sigma in Education. He has also been honoured with the President of India's National Teacher Award in the year 2006 and the Best Science Teacher State Award (By the Ministry of Science and Technology, State of UP), Innovation in Education for his inception of Six Sigma In Education by Education Watch, New Delhi and Education World- Best Teacher Award, BOLT Learner Teacher Award by Air India, 'Innovation in Education Award 2016' by Higher Education Forum (HEF), Gujarat Chapter, among others.

He has developed over 150 FREE EDUCATIONAL MOBILE Apps for the Google Play Store exclusively for Teachers, Students and Parents. This work has been recognised by the LIMCA BOOK OF RECORDS & INDIA BOOK OF RECORDS as the only Indian to draw that feast. As a premier UDEMY Instructor, he has developed over 450 UDEMY. Dr Mehrotra is presently working as a PRINCIPAL at Kunwar's Global School, Lucknow in India. He has conducted over 1000 workshops globally on

"Excellence In Education" integrated with Total Quality Management and Six Sigma, Technology Integration in Education (TIE), Developing towards being ROCKSTAR TEACHERS, including Cyberspace, Cyber Security, Classroom Management, School Leadership & Management, and Innovative teaching within classrooms via Mind Maps, NLP and Experiential Learning in Academics. He is an active TEDx speaker and can be viewed on the youtube TEDx channel. He can be visited at www.authordheerajmehrotra.com

Books By The Same Author

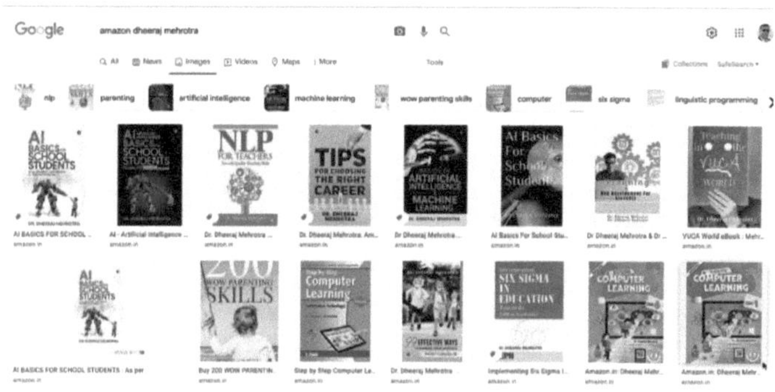

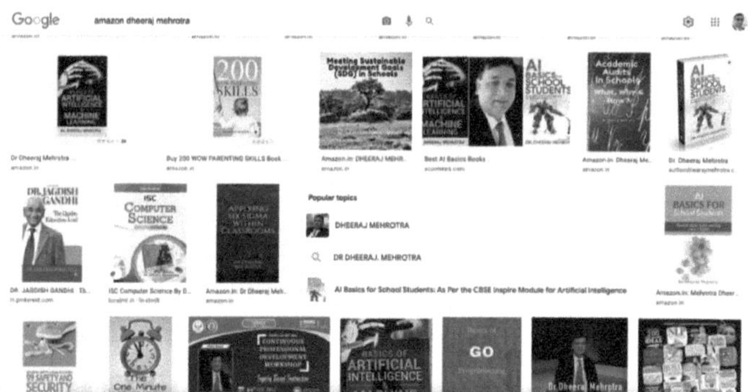

Visit: www.authordheerajmehrotra.com for more details.

Printed by Libri Plureos GmbH in Hamburg, Germany